Here's One I Wrote Earlier
Year 4

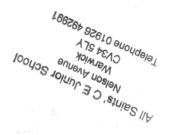

Here's One I Wrote Earlier

Instant resources for **modelled** and **shared** writing

Year 4

Gill Matthews and Gill Howell

Learning Matters

Acknowledgements

Pages 10–11: My Eyes Are Watering, ©Trevor Harvey, was first
published in Our Side of the Playground, poems
chosen by Tony Bradman, Bodley Head 1991.

First published in 2001 by Learning Matters Ltd.
Reprinted in 2002.

© Gill Matthews and Gill Howell

British Library Cataloguing in Publication Data
A CIP record for this book is available from the British Library.

ISBN 1 903300 25 8

Cover and text design by Topics – The Creative Partnership
Project management by Deer Park Productions
Typeset by Anneset, Weston-super-Mare, Somerset
Printed and bound in Great Britain by Ashford Colour Press, Gosport, Hants.

Learning Matters Ltd
58 Wonford Road
Exeter EX2 4LQ
Tel: 01392 215560
Email: info@learningmatters.co.uk
www.learningmatters.co.uk

Contents

Introduction

Here's One I Wrote Earlier, as its name suggests, offers you a substantial bank of examples of writing that you can use in modelled and shared writing sessions.

Demonstrating how to approach a particular piece of writing, or an aspect of the writing process, is an extremely effective teaching strategy. However, to think of ideas and to prepare resources for these sessions can be time consuming – and often challenging.

The examples provided here range from brief character sketches to outline playscripts, from non-fictional recounts to stories which raise issues that often concern children. These examples are aimed at different stages of development – from a planning frame, to an outline draft and then to a polished version, – so you can use them to take children through the whole writing process.

What are modelled and shared writing?

Modelled and shared writing take place during the whole-class session of the literacy hour. They are used to demonstrate specific skills and strategies used by writers. Modelled writing involves the teacher in 'creating' the piece of writing in front of the class. Shared writing is collaborative – the children make suggestions for content, choice of vocabulary, sentence construction, etc.

Children often think that experienced writers write perfectly all the time. It is important, therefore, that when using both teaching strategies, that you talk to the children about how you write (e.g. rehearsing sentences out loud before writing them down, explaining choices of particular words and phrases, discussing possible spelling options. It is useful sometimes to make mistakes – and to demonstrate how to edit and improve a piece of writing as you write.

To keep the children interested during modelled and shared writing, you could involve them by using interactive techniques e.g. asking questions, giving quick individual writing tasks on the whiteboard, taking time out for discussions, asking the children to come out to the front to write. Make sure that all the children can see – and reach – the writing surface. When appropriate, write on paper rather than a wipe-clean surface as this will mean the writing can be returned to for further work.

How to use this book

There are two ways to find appropriate writing examples in this book:

- Page v lists the contents of the book by literacy focus. Use this page to find, for example, samples of story planning or instructions.

- The grid on page ix lists the teaching objectives covered and the relevant examples of writing.

The examples are organised by term and in groups that take you through the development of a piece of writing. **All the examples in the book may be photocopied.** Some examples have been annotated so you can use them to focus on specific teaching points (for example, pages 12 and 13, 16 and 17, 20 and 21, etc.).

Each page is organised in the same way to help you find your way around each example quickly and easily. Each example is prefaced by contextual information and is linked clearly to the National Literacy Strategy (NLS) teaching objectives.

You'll also find suggested writing activities after each example:

 This indicates suggestions for teacher-led activities when working with the whole class.

 This indicates suggestions for activities the children could complete independently, either on their own, in pairs or in groups.

You may wish to remove the activities section at the bottom of the page and then enlarge the page, or make copies for use on an OHP. In some instances, you could give copies to the children for them to work on independently. Equally, you could use them for ideas and present them as if you had written them earlier!

Stimulus material

Wherever possible, the topics chosen for writing for each term have been linked to provide continuity. The examples are based on the identified range of texts for reading and writing in the NLS *Framework for Teaching,* and some non-fiction writing has links to other curricular areas (e.g. a science or history topic from the same, or earlier, term). Traditional tales and rhymes are used frequently as these provide a well-known basis that allows the children to focus on the writing process rather than be diverted by unfamiliar or challenging content.

Planning grid

To aid planning, this grid refers to word, sentence and text level teaching objectives in the NLS Framework for teaching.

Term 1

Word level	Page level	Sentence level	Page	Text level	Page
		2	4, 6, 15, 16, 17, 20, 21	9	1, 2
		3	4, 6	10	1, 2, 3
		4	4, 6	11	4, 5, 6
				12	3
				13	7, 8, 9
				14	10, 11
				24	12, 13
				25	14, 15, 16, 17
				26	16, 17
				27	18, 19, 20, 21

Term 2

Word level	Page	Sentence level	Page	Text level	Page
		1	22, 23, 24, 25, 26, 27	10	22, 23, 24, 25, 26, 27
				11	29, 30
				13	28
				14	31, 32, 33
				21	31, 32, 35
				24	34, 35, 36, 37, 38
				25	36

Term 3

Word level	Page	Sentence level	Page	Text level	Page
		4	53, 54	11	39, 40
				12	41, 42, 43, 44
				13	45, 46, 47
				14	48
				15	49, 50
				21	51, 52, 53
				22	52, 53
				23	54
				24	55, 56
				25	57, 58

Term 1 Fiction

Story planning Planning frame (version 1 – see also page 3)
Main focus Making notes
NLS teaching objectives T9, T10

Characters

Setting

Beginning

Problem

Ending

Activities

 • Use the planning frame to demonstrate how to make notes about a story.

 • Use the planning frame to make own notes about a story.

Term 1 Fiction

Story planning Planning frame (version 2)
Main focus Making notes
NLS teaching objectives T9, T10

Beginning

Who?

What?

Why?

Problem

Who?

What?

Why?

Ending

Who?

What?

Why?

Activities

 • Use the planning frame to demonstrate how to make notes about a story.

 • Use the planning frame to make own notes about a story.

Term 1 Fiction

Historical story
Main focus Completed planning frame
(version 1 – see also page 1)
NLS teaching objectives T10, T12

Characters
Margaret and Marion
Both in same class at school
Eight-year-olds

Setting
School
Air-raid shelter

Beginning
Margaret and Marion at school
Doing lessons
Tired due to interrupted night because of air raids

Problem
Air-raid siren starts going off
Put on gas masks
Have to go into air-raid shelter

Ending
All-clear sounds
Come out of shelter
Discover that school has been bombed and destroyed
Margaret and Marion pleased – no more school

Activity

- Use as a model to demonstrate how to plan a historical story.

Term 1 Fiction

Character sketches
Main focus Completed plan (see also page 5)
NLS teaching objectives S2, S3, S4, T11

Character's name and personal details
Miss Cane – school teacher

Appearance
Tall and thin
Brown hair scraped back into a bun
Pointed nose
Black eyes set close together. Peers over steel-rimmed glasses
Always wears black or grey clothes

Personality
Mean. Seems to dislike children
Bully

Movement
Walks quickly with small steps
Clicks her fingers to attract attention
Verbs: strides, slams, throws
Adverbs: forcefully, purposefully

Speech
Verbs: snaps, barks, sneers, shouts
Adverbs: gruffly, spitefully, abruptly

Activities

- Use as a model to demonstrate how to plan a character sketch.
- Discuss how identifying how you want the reader to feel about the character helps with the plan.

- Focus on the choice of vocabulary.

**Term 1
Fiction**

Character sketches Planning frame
Main focus Making notes (see also page 4)
NLS teaching objective T11

Character's name and personal details

Appearance

Personality

Movememment
Verbs:

Adverbs:

Speech
Verbs:

Adverbs:

Activities

- Use as a framework to plan a character sketch.

- Use as a framework to plan own character sketches.

Term 1 Fiction

Character sketches
Main focus Model text
NLS teaching objectives S2, S3, S4, T11

Miss Cane threw open the door and strode forcefully into the classroom. She gripped her chalk so hard it broke into two pieces, showering the front row with chalk dust.

'Who,' she snapped, 'has been trampling all over my flower bed?' She glared around the classroom, her eyes glittering icily behind her steel-rimmed glasses.

'Charlie Jackson,' she sneered, 'come out here.'

She held Charlie's shoulder tightly and spoke through clenched teeth, her thin lips turning white. 'Show me the soles of your shoes.'

Activities

- Use as a model to demonstrate how to write a character sketch using the notes on page 4.
- Focus on vocabulary that evokes feelings about, and responses to, the character.
- Discuss the effect of adverbs on the writing.
- Discuss the choice of name for this character.

- Draw an illustration of Miss Cane.

Term 1 Fiction

Playscripts
Main focus Draft for improvement
NLS teaching objective T13

Little Miss Muffet

Narrator: One day, Little Miss Muffet went out for a walk. It was a lovely day so she decided to sit down in the sunshine.

Little Miss Muffet: I'm feeling quite peckish after my long walk. I'll see what Mum has packed in my lunchbox. Oh no! Curds and whey again!

Narrator: Even though Miss Muffet wasn't very keen on curds and whey, she started to eat. Suddenly, she felt something tickling her cheek. It was a spider and Miss Muffet hated spiders.

Little Miss Muffet: Aaaagh!

Narrator: Miss Muffet ran home screaming.

Activities

- Focus on how the narrator is telling the story.

- Explore how more of the story could be told through dialogue and the use of stage directions (see page 8).

Term 1 Fiction

Playscripts
Main focus Improved draft
NLS teaching objective T13

Little Miss Muffet

Narrator: One day, Little Miss Muffet went out for a walk.

Little Miss Muffet: What a lovely day. I'm feeling quite peckish after my long walk. I think I'll sit in the sunshine on this tuffet and see what Mum has packed in my lunchbox.

Miss Muffet (peers into her lunchbox.): Oh no! Curds and whey again!

Narrator: Even though Miss Muffet wasn't very keen on curds and whey, she started to eat.

Miss Muffet (touching her cheek): What's that tickling my cheek?

Narrator: It was a spider and Miss Muffet hated spiders.

Little Miss Muffet (throws her lunchbox into the air and screams): Mum! Mum!

Narrator: Miss Muffet ran home.

Activities

- Focus on how the dialogue is telling most of the story.
- Discuss what the stage directions add to the play.
- Compare the original draft (page 7) with this improved version.

- Write the next scene when Miss Muffet tells her mum what happened.

Term 1 Fiction

Playscript
Main focus Model text
NLS teaching objective T13

Miss Muffet and the Spider

Narrator: Little Miss Muffet was eating her curds and whey when suddenly she noticed a large spider.

Miss Muffet: Hello, Mr Spider! How are you today?

Spider: I'm really hungry. What are you eating?

Miss Muffet (sighing): It's curds and whey again. I really don't like it but it's all my mum can make.

Spider (licking his lips): Curds and whey? Yummy! Tell you what, if I go and get my friend the Bee, will you swap your curds and whey for some of his honey?

Miss Muffet: Oh yes, I love honey!

(*Spider rushes off and returns with the Bee.*)

The Bee: Here you are, have some of my honey.

Miss Muffet: Thank you, Bee. Oh, but I've nothing to put the honey on. I need some bread.

The Bee: I'll go and get my friend the Farmer. We'll swap some of my honey for some of his bread.

(*The Bee buzzes off and returns with the Farmer.*)

Activities

- Explain that this playscript innovates upon the nursery rhyme *Little Miss Muffet*: the same main characters have been used but the plot has changed.
- Discuss further characters who might appear.

- Write the next scene in this play.

Term 1 Poetry

Personal experience *Something that Upset Me*
Main focus Drafting
NLS teaching objective T14

Something that Upset Me

My teacher once said that I must try harder with my writing.
She said that my handwriting was untidy, my spelling wasn't good
and I hadn't used interesting words.
I had lots of ideas but they just wouldn't come out of my head.

Activities

- The ideas on this page and the next are based on the poem *My Eyes are Watering* by Trevor Harvey. If possible, read this to the children to use it as a stimulus for writing further poems.
- Explain you are going to write down a few ideas about a time when you were upset at school.

- Write about an upsetting time at school or at home.

Term 1 Poetry

Personal experience
Main focus Model text
NLS teaching objective T14

My Eyes Are Watering

I've got a cold
And that is why
My eyes are watering.

It's nothing to do
With Mrs Smith
Shouting about my work.
Inside my head
Good ideas wriggle around
But I can't quite catch them
On the paper.
My writing staggers across the page.
Letters muddle and scramble.
Adjectives and powerful verbs fade away.

Look at her –
She's having a cry!
Not true.
I've got a cold
And THAT is why
My eyes are watering.

OK?

Activities

- Discuss the changes made in this draft based on the original notes (see page 10) and on the original poem by Trevor Harvey.

- Use notes to write poems about upsetting experiences.

Term 1 Non-fiction

Newspaper articles
Main focus Model text (see also page 13)
NLS teaching objective T24

SCREAM A-WHEY!

A local spider is resting in hospital following a frightening event involving a small girl.

From his hospital bed, his head wrapped in bandages, the spider said: 'I was minding my own business up in the tree by the tuffet in the park. I thought I could smell curds and whey so I decided to slip down my web for a scout round. The next thing I knew I was being screamed at. I think it was that Muffet girl, she's got a thing about spiders, she screamed and screamed and would not stop. My ears are still ringing, I can tell you. I can't hear a thing.'

A spokesperson for the Society for the Protection of Spiders told our reporter, Tara N. Tula, that this kind of event is becoming increasingly common: 'What is the world coming to when an innocent spider can't move around his own web?' she asked.

Police investigating the incident wish to interview Miss Muffet, aged 9, who has often been seen eating curds and whey in the park.

Activities

- Discuss the format of the article. Focus on the headline and the use of word play.
- Write alternative headlines for the article.

- Write newspaper articles based on other known rhymes and poems.

Term 1
Non-fiction

Newspaper articles
Main focus Annotated model text (see also page 12)
NLS teaching objective T24

SCREAM A-WHEY!

Introduction

Headline using word play

A local spider is resting in hospital following a frightening event involving a small girl.

From his hospital bed, his head wrapped in bandages, the spider said: 'I was minding my own business up in the tree by the tuffet in the park. I thought I could smell curds and whey so I decided to slip down my web for a scout round. The next thing I knew I was being screamed at. I think it was that Muffet girl, she's got a thing about spiders, she screamed and screamed and would not stop. My ears are still ringing, I can tell you. I can't hear a thing.'

Details

A spokesperson for the Society for the Protection of Spiders told our reporter, Tara N. Tula, that this kind of event is becoming increasingly common: 'What is the world coming to when an innocent spider can't move around his own web?' she asked.

Police investigating the incident wish to interview Miss Muffet, aged 9, who has often been seen eating curds and whey in the park.

Details

Personal information

Closing sentence

Personal opinion

Fact

Activities

- Discuss the format of the article. Focus on the headline and the use of word play.
- Write alternative headlines for the article.

- Write newspaper articles based on other known rhymes and poems.

Term 1
Non-fiction

Instructions Planning frame
Main focus Making notes (see page 15)
NLS teaching objective T25

Title

Equipment

Method

Activity

• Use the planning frame to demonstrate how to plan instructions.

14

Term 1
Non-fiction

Instructions
Main focus Draft for improvement (see page 14)
NLS teaching objectives S2, T25

A spider

Equipment
You first have to go and get a black glove, some buttons and a sewing needle and some cotton thread to sew with.

Method
First you will need to put the glove on to check where the buttons should go. The buttons are going to be the eyes. Once you have decided where to put the buttons, make a mark. Sew on the buttons with the cotton. Put on the glove and move your hand like a spider. You can decorate your spider puppet with wool for hair or felt or other stuff like that.

Activities

- Focus on the style and layout of these instructions. Discuss how they could be improved. Through shared writing, make any necessary changes.
- Identify and delete any unnecessary words.
- Discuss the choice of verbs.

- List alternative verbs that could be used instead of 'Put'.

Term 1
Non-fiction

Instructions
Main focus Model text (see also page 17)
NLS teaching objectives S2, T25, T26

Making a spider puppet

Equipment
1 black glove
2 buttons for eyes
A sewing needle
Sewing cotton
Wool, felt or other material for decoration

Method
1. Put on the glove
2. Ask a friend to mark the position of the eyes
3. Take off the glove and sew on the eyes
4. Decorate the puppet with wool, felt or other material
5. Practise moving your puppet like a spider

Activity

 • Use as a model to demonstrate how to improve draft instructions.

Term 1
Non-fiction

Instructions
Main focus Annotated model text (see also page 16)
NLS teaching objectives S2, T25, T26

Making a spider puppet

Equipment

① black glove — Specific quantities
② buttons for eyes
A sewing needle
Sewing cotton
Wool, felt or other material for decoration

List in order of use

Present tense. Verbs at the beginning of the sentence

Method

1. Put on the glove
2. Ask a friend to mark the position of the eyes
3. Take off the glove and sew on the eyes
4. Decorate the puppet with wool, felt or other material
5. Practise moving your puppet like a spider

Sequenced instructions

Action verbs, 2nd person

Activity

• Use as a model to demonstrate how to improve draft instructions.

Term 1
Non-fiction

Reports Planning frame
Main focus Making notes (see also page 19)
NLS teaching objective T27

Introduction

Appearance

Habitat

Feeding habits

Fascinating facts

Activity

 • Use the frame to plan a report about an animal.

Term 1
Non-fiction

Reports
Main focus Completed plan (see page 18)
NLS teaching objective T27

Introduction
House spiders – Latin name – *Tegenaria domestica*
Originally from warmer countries – Spain

Appearance
Females 9-10 mm
Males 6-9 mm
Yellowish-grey

Habitat
Live in houses all year
Make webs in corners of rooms
Females can live up to 4 years
Seen more often in late summer and autumn – houses warm and dry, also males out searching for mates

Feeding habits
Flies, furniture beetles

Fascinating facts
Males can run up to 50 cm/sec
Spiders thought to be lucky. If you wish to live and thrive, let the spider run alive

Activities

- Use to demonstrate how to complete a plan for a report. Focus on the use of key words and phrases as used in notes.
- Discuss alternative headings for other report plans.

**Term 1
Non-fiction**

Reports
Main focus Model text (see also page 21)
NLS teaching objectives S2, T27

House spiders

The Latin name for house spiders is *Tegenaria domestica.* It is thought they came to Britain in the holds of ships from warm countries such as Spain.

Female house spiders are 9–10 mm in length, males are slightly smaller, measuring 6–9 mm. Both males and females look similar and are yellowy-grey in colour.

House spiders live in our houses all year round although we tend to see more of them in late summer and the autumn. This is because more of them come indoors as the weather becomes colder and wetter. Also, the males are out searching for mates. House spiders spin and live in webs in the corner of rooms. Females can live for as long as 4 years.

Spiders eat insects such as flies and beetles. They help keep down the number of unwanted insects in our homes.

Many people think that spiders are lucky and that they should not be killed. This belief is told in an old rhyme: 'If you wish to live and thrive, let the spider run alive.'

Activities

- Use the model to demonstrate how to turn notes into continuous text.
- Discuss why reports such as this one are written in the present tense.

Term 1
Non-fiction

Reports
Main focus Annotated model text (see also page 20)
NLS teaching objectives S2, T27

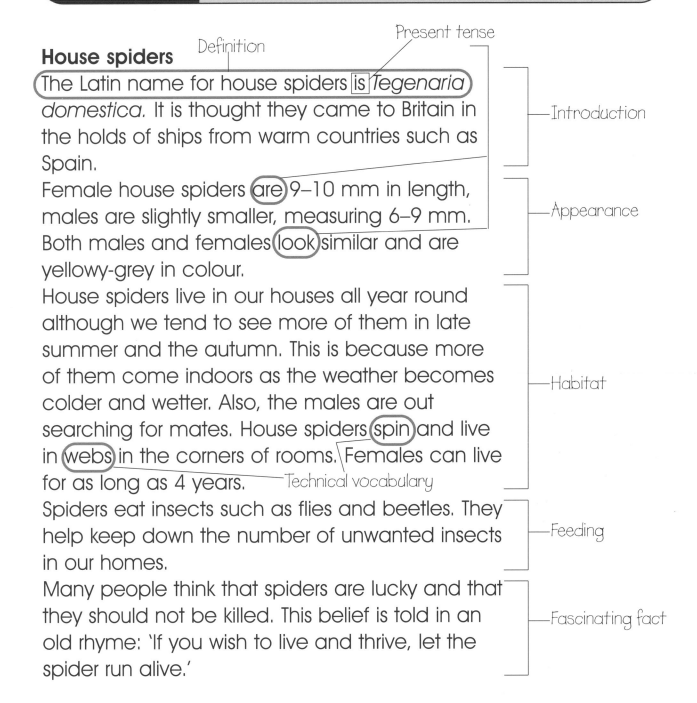

House spiders

Definition

Present tense

The Latin name for house spiders is *Tegenaria domestica.* It is thought they came to Britain in the holds of ships from warm countries such as Spain.

—— Introduction

Female house spiders are 9–10 mm in length, males are slightly smaller, measuring 6–9 mm. Both males and females look similar and are yellowy-grey in colour.

—— Appearance

House spiders live in our houses all year round although we tend to see more of them in late summer and the autumn. This is because more of them come indoors as the weather becomes colder and wetter. Also, the males are out searching for mates. House spiders spin and live in webs in the corners of rooms. Females can live for as long as 4 years.

Technical vocabulary

—— Habitat

Spiders eat insects such as flies and beetles. They help keep down the number of unwanted insects in our homes.

—— Feeding

Many people think that spiders are lucky and that they should not be killed. This belief is told in an old rhyme: 'If you wish to live and thrive, let the spider run alive.'

—— Fascinating fact

Activities

- Use the model to demonstrate how to turn notes into continuous text.
- Discuss why reports such as this one are written in the present tense.

**Term 2
Fiction**

Familiar settings
Main focus Figurative language (see also page 22)
NLS teaching objectives S1, T10

An icy East wind swept the playground. Crumpled and discarded

crisp packets danced with the children on the grey tarmac, each

more wildly than the next. Brittle fingers of rain began to prod the

children's cheeks and small groups huddled together

like old gossiping women.

Activities

- Discuss the use of metaphor, simile, adjectival and adverbial phrases.

- Ask the children to identify the senses of sight, sound, smell and touch.

Term 2 Fiction

Familiar settings
Main focus Figurative language (see also page 22)
NLS teaching objectives S1, T10

An (icy East) wind swept the playground. (Crumpled) and (discarded)

Adjectives   Adjective   Adjective

crisp packets (danced with the children) on the grey tarmac, each

Figurative

(more wildly than the next.) (Brittle) fingers of (rain began to prod)

Adverbial phrase   Adjective   Metaphor

the children's cheeks and small groups huddled together

Simile

(like old gossiping women.)

Activities

- Discuss use of metaphor, simile, adjectival and adverbial phrases.

- Ask the children to identify the senses of sight, sound, smell and touch.

Term 2 Fiction

Familiar settings
Main focus Figurative language, adjectives and similes
(see also page 25)
NLS teaching objectives S1, T10

As the sun rose on the grey city streets, the hum of traffic and

people-noise grew and swelled like a swarm of angry bees

approaching. Above the streets, sparkling starlings chattered in

tree tops, and peaceful pigeons cooed contentedly at the start of

another day. The narrow pavements filled with people.

Activities

- Discuss the use of simile, adjectives and alliterative phrases.
- Use as the stimulus for further writing of settings.

- Write own familiar settings.

Term 2 Fiction

Familiar settings
Main focus Figurative language, adjectives and similes
(see also page 24)
NLS teaching objectives S1, T10

As the sun rose on the (grey) city streets, the hum of traffic and
Adjective

(people-noise) grew and swelled (like a swarm of angry bees)
Figurative   Simile

approaching. Above the streets, (sparkling) starlings chattered in
Adjective

tree tops, and (peaceful) pigeons (cooed contentedly) at the start of
Adjective   Alliterative phrase

another day. The narrow pavements filled with people.

Activities

- Discuss the use of simile, adjectives and alliterative phrases.
- Use as the stimulus for further writing of settings.

- Write own familiar settings.

**Term 2
Fiction**

Familiar settings
Main focus Model text (see also page 27)
NLS teaching objectives S1, T10

The shingle beach glistened in the weak sunlight, as the

waves slid the pebbles around on the shore. High above the sea,

gulls were soaring in the blue sky, hovering on the warm air

like kites. At the high-tide line, there came the strong, salty

smell as drying seaweed decorated the stones in green,

brown and bronze fronds.

Activity

 • Use as a model to demonstrate how to write effective settings.

**Term 2
Fiction**

Familiar settings
Main focus Annotated model text (see also page 26)
NLS teaching objectives S2, T10

The (shingle) beach glistened in the (weak) sunlight, as the

Adjective   Adjective

(waves slid the pebbles) around on the shore. High above the sea,

Figurative

gulls were soaring in the (blue) sky, hovering on the (warm) air

Adjective   Adjective

(like kites.) At the high-tide line, there came the (strong, salty)

Simile   Adjectives

smell as drying seaweed (decorated the stones) in

Figurative

(green, brown and bronze) fronds.

Adjectives

Activity

• Use as a model to demonstrate how to write effective settings.

Term 2 Fiction

Familiar settings Planning frame
Main focus Making notes
NLS teaching objective T13

Setting

Sight	Sound
Smell	Touch

Activities

 • Use the grid to describe the settings of stories you have read.

 • Use adjectives and similes.

Term 2 Poetry

Classic poems *Monday's Child*
Main focus Poetry based on structure/style of poems read
(model poem) (see also page 30)
NLS teaching objective T11

Monday's child is fair of face
Tuesday's child is full of grace
Wednesday's child is full of woe
Thursday's child has far to go
Friday's child is loving and giving
Saturday's child works hard for a living
But the child that is born on the Sabbath day
Is bonnie, blithe, good and gay.

Activity

- Use this as a model poem and highlight the features to retain when writing a new version.

Term 2 Poetry

Classic poems
Main focus Model of a new version of poem (see also page 29)
NLS teaching objective T11

Monday's cat is far too fluffy
Tuesday's cat is old and scruffy
Wednesday's cat is such a fright
Thursday's cat howls through the night
Friday's cat is much too frisky
Saturdays cat steals Grandad's whisky
But the cat that comes on the Sabbath day
Is pretty and perfect in every way.

Activities

 • Refer to the repeated pattern of key words and to the rhyming scheme.

 • Write own version of Monday's child.

**Term 2
Non-fiction**

Note-making
Main focus Making notes and editing (see also page 32)
NLS teaching objectives T14, T21

These are the rules for this school

When you come into the classroom, you may talk quietly while you hang your coats on the pegs. You should put your lunchboxes under the bench by the wall, if you bring sandwiches, that is. If you don't, put your dinner money envelopes into the tray on the teacher's desk. You should bring it on Mondays. Sit down at your place while the teacher takes the register, and answer your name. If you are absent, don't answer, but bring a note on return. Then line up quietly before going into the hall. You go into the hall for assembly.

Activity

• Use as a model to show how to delete unnecessary words in instructions.

Term 2
Non-fiction

Note-making
Main focus Making notes and editing (see also page 31)
NLS teaching objectives T14, T21

~~These are the~~ rules ~~for this~~ school   *School Rules*

~~When you come into the classroom, you may~~ talk quietly while you hang ~~your~~ coats on ~~the~~ pegs. ~~You should put your~~ lunchboxes under ~~the~~ bench ~~by the wall, if you bring sandwiches, that is. If you don't,~~ put ~~your~~ dinner money ~~envelopes~~ into the tray on ~~the teacher's desk. You should bring it in on~~ Mondays. Sit down ~~at your place while the teacher takes~~ the register, ~~and answer your name.~~ If ~~you are~~ absent, ~~don't answer, but~~ bring a note on return ~~instead. Then~~ line up quietly ~~before going into the hall. You go into the hall~~ for assembly.

Activity

- Use as a model to show how to delete unnecessary words in instructions.

Term 2
Non-fiction

Note-making
Main focus Summarising (edited version)
NLS teaching objective T14

School rules

Talk quietly
Hang coats on pegs
Lunchboxes go under bench
On Mondays, put dinner money in tray on desk
Sit down for the register
If absent, bring a note on return
Line up quietly for assembly

Activity

 • Draw attention to command verbs, the format of a list and the lack of
unnecessary words.

Term 2
Non-fiction

Explanation Planning frame
Main focus Making notes (see also page 35)
NLS teaching objective T24

Definition

Sequenced explanation
First . . .

Next . . .

Then . . .

This causes . . .

Finally . . .

Fascinating fact

Activities

- Use to make notes to structure an explanation.

- Use the planning frame to make own notes.

Term 2
Non-fiction

Explanation
Main focus Completed planning frame (see also page 34)
NLS teaching objectives T21, T24

Definition Bungee jumping is a hobby some people do for fun.

Sequenced explanation

First, they climb up to the top of a tower.

Next, they tie a strong stretchy cord to their feet.

Then they jump off.

This causes the cord to stretch and then spring back.

Finally, the person hangs, bouncing as the cord returns to its original shape.

Fascinating fact

Bungee jumping was first done by young men on the island of Vanuatu. They tied vines to their ankles and jumped from bamboo towers.

Activities

 • Draw attention to the use of connectives to structure the sequence of an explanation.

 • Collect and record other time connectives.

The why and how of bungee jumping

Bungee jumping is a hobby some people do for pleasure. They jump off a bridge or a crane from a great height, with a piece of stretchy cord attached to their legs. It is tied firmly to the object being jumped off. The person falls the length of the cord, then bounces back when the cord reaches the end of its stretch. First, the person climbs up to the top. The cord, which must be strong but stretchy, is fixed to their ankles. They jump off. As they fall, their weight stretches out the cord. When it is fully stretched, it springs back. It is important the spring in the cord is strong enough to return to its original shape. Heavier people have more bounces than light ones, because they make the cord stretch further, so it is harder to return to its original length. The cord must not be too long, or the bungee jumper will hit the ground.

The first jump in England took place on April Fool's Day 1979.

**Term 2
Non-fiction**

Explanation
Main focus Model text (see also page 38)
NLS teaching objective T24

The why and how of bungee jumping

An unusual hobby

Bungee jumping is an unusual hobby which some people do for fun.

How bungee jumping works

First, the person climbs up to the top of a tower. A cord, which must be strong but stretchy, is fixed to their ankles. Then they jump off. Their weight stretches out the cord until it is fully stretched. Then it springs back.

- It is important the cord has a strong enough spring to return to its original shape.
- The cord must not be too long, or the bungee jumper will hit the ground.

Heavier people bounce more than light ones. This is because they cause the cord to stretch further, so it is harder to return to its original length.

The first jump in England took place on April Fool's Day 1979

Activities

- Use as a model to demonstrate how to write an explanation.
- Identify the linking phrases, the layout, etc.

- In pairs, identify changes made to the original draft (page 36) and record why you think the changes were made.

Term 2
Non-fiction

Explanation Bungee jumping
Main focus Annotated model text (see also page 37)
NLS teaching objective T24

The why and how of bungee jumping —— Main heading

An unusual hobby ———— Sub heading

Bungee jumping is an unusual hobby which some people do for fun.

General description

How bungee jumping works

Sub heading

First, the person climbs up to the top of a tower. A cord, which must be strong but stretchy, is fixed to their ankles. ———— Connectives

Then they jump off. Their weight stretches out the cord until it is fully stretched. Then it springs back.

- It is important the cord has a strong enough spring to return to its original shape. | Bullet points of technical information |
- The cord must not be too long, or the bungee jumper will hit the ground.

Cause and effect

Heavier people bounce more than light ones. This is because they cause the cord to stretch further, so it is harder to return to its original length.

The first jump took place in England on April Fool's Day 1979. — Fascinating fact

Activities

- Use as a model to demonstrate how to write an explanation.
- Identify the linking phrases, the layout, etc.

- In pairs, identify changes made to the original draft (page 36) and record why you think the changes were made.

Term 3 Fiction

Stories that raise issues
Main focus Drafting
NLS teaching objective T11

Issue Bullying

Boy sees two of his friends bullying a younger child and taking his dinner money. What should he do?

Dilemma

1. Confront the bullies and get back the dinner money.
2. Tell one of the teachers.
3. Ignore it.
4. Join in.

Story opening – Describe the scene: who, what, why?

Prompt questions

- Should it be first or third person?

- Think about the results that might happen if the boy takes any of the options.

- What are his feelings/fears?

Activity

 • Use the discussion points to plan writing the story.

Term 3 Fiction

Stories that raise issues Planning frame
Main focus Making notes
NLS teaching objective T11

Issue/dilemma

Opening scene (describe the characters and setting)

What'll happen if . . . ?

Action of main character

Outcome/feelings – (good or bad?)

Ending (moral?)

Activities

 • Use these headings to plan a story with the class.

 • Use the headings to draft own story.

Term 3 Fiction

Alternative versions of well-known stories
Main focus Alternative ending
NLS teaching objective T12

The Three Billy Goats Gruff

After the second billy goat crossed over the rickety-rackety bridge to the green grass, the third and biggest billy goat went trip, trap, trip, trap over the bridge.

'Oh ho!' cried the evil troll again. 'Now I'm going to eat you up!'

Big Billy Goat Gruff lowered his horns and charged at the troll, cheered on by his little brothers.

'Go! Big Billy!' they cried with glee.

Then, just as Big Billy Goat Gruff reached him, the troll stepped neatly to the side, and the billy goat went flying off the bridge and crashed on to the rocks below.

'Dinner!' gloated the troll, and set about skinning the goat for his pot. 'I'll have this big one for my main course, and then those two little wimps for dessert.'

The troll enjoyed the best meal he had eaten in a long time and, at last, no one tramped over his bridge to disturb his sleep.

Activities

- Draw attention to the similarities and differences between this version and the original story.

- In pairs, discuss and record how your view of the original story has changed.

Term 3 Fiction

Alternative versions of well-known stories
Main focus Alternative ending
NLS teaching objective T12

The Princess and the Pea

When the princess went to the guest room to sleep, she saw the huge pile of mattresses on the bed.

'So, it's the old "Pea in the bed" trick,' she thought. 'That must mean the prince is looking for a bride!'

The princess did not want to get married yet, and certainly not to this dull prince and his interfering mother, so she decided to trick them too. As the pea would make the bed too uncomfortable for sleep, she heaved one mattress on to the floor and slept peacefully. In the morning, when the Queen asked her how she had slept, the princess replied:

'I have never had such a dreadful night!'

The queen looked hopefully at her son. The prince smiled.

'At last, a real princess,' he thought.

'I fell off the top of the bed,' continued the princess, 'I banged my head, and bruised my arm, and I am going straight home!'

The princess laughed as she left, and vowed to tell all her princess-friends about the trick.

No more princesses called at the castle on stormy nights, and the prince and his mother, the queen, were forced to live together for the rest of their lives.

Activities

- Draw attention to the similarities and differences between this version and the original story.

- In pairs, discuss and record how your view of the original story has changed.

42

Term 3 Fiction

Alternative versions of well-known stories
Main focus Alternative ending
NLS teaching objective T12

Cinderella

When the prince arrived at the home of the Ugly Sisters, he saw that the little glass slipper fitted the ugliest one, called Nelly. He was dismayed. But he had given his word. He had promised to marry whoever the tiny slipper that was left behind at the ball fitted .

‘She looked so pretty at the ball,’ he mused with sadness, ‘I would rather marry that scruffy kitchen maid than Ugly Nelly.’

As Nelly took his hand, she looked up at the sky and said thank you to her fairy godmother.

‘That new spell really worked. Cinderella’s feet grew big and mine grew small. We tricked everyone. Now I’ll live happily ever after.’

Activities

- Draw attention to the similarities and differences between this version and the original story.

- In pairs, discuss and record how your view of the original story has changed.

Term 3 Fiction

Alternative versions of well-known stories Planning frame
Main focus Making notes
NLS teaching objective T12

Original story title

Point at which to make a change in the ending

How the alteration affects
Characters

Setting

Outcome

Activities

 • Use to plan an alternative ending to a well-known story.

 • Use the frame to plan an alternative ending to a well-known story.

Term 3 Fiction

Story planning
Main focus Model story plan in chapters (see also page 46)
NLS teaching objective T13

Chapter 1

Who, what, where, why?

Mr and Mrs O'Connell bought a new camper van to take their children on a touring holiday of the Lake District. Their youngest son is called Liam. They were excited and eager to set off.

Add – feelings, descriptions of character, camper van, weather, etc.

Chapter 2

Problem occurs

After the van is packed and ready to go, Mr O'Connell drops the key. It falls into a drain.

Add: feelings, conversation, ideas to solve problem, sense of disappointment, blame, time passing by.

Chapter 3

Actions to solve the problem

They try to lift the drain cover.

They try to use a bent coat hanger to hook it. It knocks key further away. The children get upset.

Mrs O'Connell makes a cup of tea to cheer everyone up.

They wait for the Fire Brigade or a car-rescue service. It takes ages to arrive.

Add: dialogue, details of setting.

Chapter 4

Resolution and close

Liam hangs a magnet on a string down the drain and gets the key, before the rescue service arrives. Everyone is amazed at how clever he is. They all have a cup of tea, and at last set off as the sun comes out.

Add: detail of thoughts, dialogue.

Activities

 • Use as a model to show how to arrange episodes into chapters.

 • Use these notes to write the full story.

Term 3 Fiction

Story planning Planning frame (1)
Main focus Making notes (see also page 45)
NLS teaching objective T13

Chapter 1
Who, what, where, why?

Chapter 2
Problem occurs

Chapter 3
Actions to solve the problem

Chapter 4
Resolution and close

Activity

- Use the planning frame as a model to structure a plan for chapters.

Term 3 Fiction

Story planning Planning frame (2)
Main focus Organise notes from a brainstorming session
NLS teaching objective T13

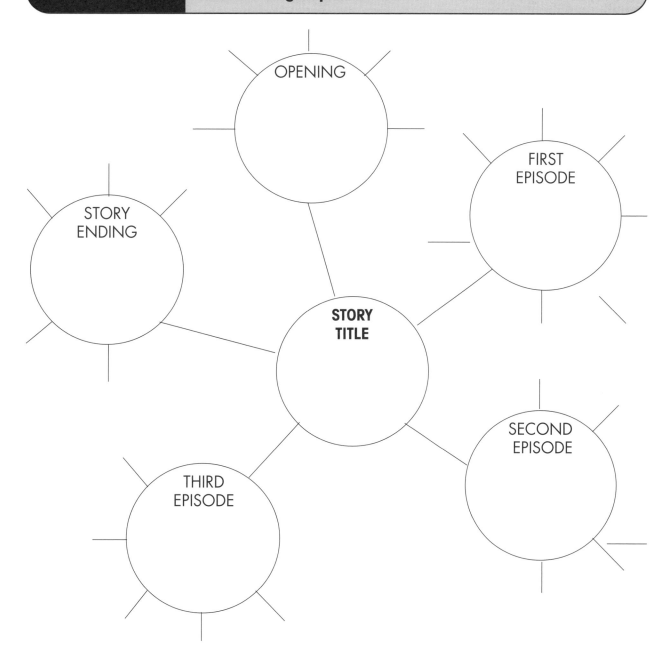

Activities

 • Use to illustrate how to organise notes from a brainstorming session and how to collaborate to write stories in chapters. Add names of children to leader lines for each episode to show who will write each episode.

 • Collaborate to write episodes in a story.

Term 3 Poetry

Different styles Same topic/theme in different styles
Main focus Model text
NLS teaching objective T14

Limerick

There was a young sparrow from Leek
Who hadn't found food for a week.
He got thinner and thinner
Without eating dinner
That skinny young sparrow from Leek.

Haiku

Small fluffed-up sparrow
Feathers fat against the frost
Frozen thin pickings

Ode

Oh Sparrow, cold in winter frost,
Do not despair of sun.
Look to the East at daybreak.
See, Spring has just begun.

Couplets

There was a little sparrow
Who found a bow and arrow.
He shot it in the sky
And it flew up very high.

Activity

- Examine the structure and form of poems on the same subject and discuss which form best suits the topic or theme.

**Term 3
Poetry**

Editing
Main focus Polishing (see also page 50)
NLS teaching objective T15

Wet black line over the earth

Across the fields and hills

It takes cars to different places

And people on their way

To visit or to work

Lorries go to and fro

As the road bears their weight

Activities

- Discuss the rhythm, rhyme, imagery and choice of vocabulary.
- Use as a draft for editing and improving.

Term 3
Poetry

Editing
Main focus Polishing (see also page 49)
NLS teaching objective T15

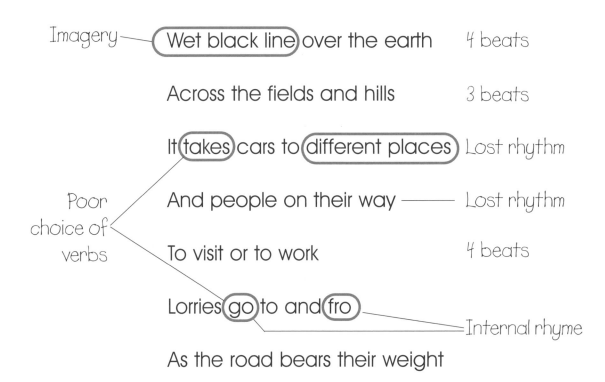

Imagery —— (Wet black line) over the earth   4 beats

Across the fields and hills   3 beats

It (takes) cars to (different places)   Lost rhythm

And people on their way ——   Lost rhythm

Poor
choice of
verbs

To visit or to work   4 beats

Lorries (go) to and (fro)   —— Internal rhyme

As the road bears their weight

Activities

• Discuss the rhythm, rhyme, imagery and choice of vocabulary.
• Use as a draft for editing and improving.

Term 3
Non-fiction

Persuasive writing
Main focus Brainstorming ideas for one point of view
NLS teaching objective T21

Easy to
decide what
to wear

Common
identity

Smart   Neat

However   **School
Uniform**   Cheaper

Because   Scruffy

No choice

Fashion   Groups on   Sports
victims   school trips   matches
can be
identified
easily   Tidy

Activity

- Add to the list using children's suggestions and organise the list in a logical order.

Term 3
Non-fiction

Persuasive writing Planning frame
Main focus Making notes (see also page 53)
NLS teaching objectives T21, T22

Statement of issue
We believe that . . .

Supporting statements
First

Secondly

Also

Opposing statement
Some people think that . . .

Return to viewpoint
However . . .

Conclusion/summary of main points

Activities

 • Use as a model of how to structure the main points of view discussed during a brainstorming session.

 • Use the frame to structure own persuasive writing.

Term 3
Non-fiction

Persuasive writing
Main focus Completed planning frame (see also page 52)
NLS teaching objectives S4, T21, T22

Statement of issue
We believe that . . .
Wearing school uniform is a good thing.

Supporting statements
First
We wouldn't have to decide what to wear every day.

Secondly
We would look smarter when we are on school trips.

Also
Our parents wouldn't need to spend so much on trendy clothes.

Opposing statement
Some people think that . . .
It takes away our freedom of choice.

Return to viewpoint
However . . .
We can still make choices outside school.

Conclusion
We all feel a uniform is the best choice.

Activities

- Use as a model of how to structure the main points of view discussed during a brainstorming session.

- Add further details to the plan.

Term 3
Non-fiction

Persuasive writing
Main focus Model text (letter)
NLS teaching objectives S4, T23

[*school address and class details here*]

[*date*]

To the Governors of _____ school

<u>Wearing a school uniform</u>

Dear Governors

We, the pupils in Year 4, wish to tell you our views in support of wearing a school uniform.

We believe that wearing school uniform is good.

First, having a school uniform will mean we won't need to waste time in the morning deciding what to wear, so we won't be late anymore.
Secondly, when we go on school trips, we will give a tidy, neat image to other people, and make it easier for the teachers to keep track of us.
We also think it will be cheaper for our parents. They won't have to buy lots of clothes to keep up with fashion while we are at school.

Some people believe that a school uniform takes away your individuality and freedom of choice. However, we think we can still make our own choices when we are outside school.

In conclusion, we feel a school uniform is the best choice for us all.

Yours faithfully

Activity

• Use as a model to demonstrate the layout of a letter and how the plan (page 53) has been turned into complete text.

Term 3
Non-fiction

Persuasive writing
Main focus Model text (paragraph) (see also page 56)
NLS teaching objective T24

I don't want to wear a school uniform because I like to look

different from every one else. I want to choose which colours I

wear, and make up my own mind. I like to look trendy, and get

the latest clothes. My mum says a school uniform is too expensive.

She says they are made from cheap material which wears out

quickly. My Dad says it is taking away my personal freedom.

Activity

• Identify the key ideas and summarise these as bullet points beneath the text.

Term 3
Non-fiction

Persuasive writing
Main focus Annotated model text (paragraph) (see also page 55)
NLS teaching objective T24

I don't want to wear a school uniform because

Individuality

(I like to look different) from every one else. (I want to choose)

Choice

which colours I wear, and make up my own mind.

Fashion

(I like to look trendy,) and get the latest clothes. My mum says a

Cost

school uniform is (too expensive.) (She says) they are made from

Opinion

(cheap material which wears out quickly.) My Dad says it is taking

Value

away my (personal freedom.) — *Choice*

Activity

- Identify the key areas and summarise these as bullet points beneath the text.

Term 3
Non-fiction

Persuasive writing
Main focus Planning a poster (see also page 58)
NLS teaching objective T25

What is its purpose?	Who is the audience?
How will we catch attention?	**Vocabulary**
What layout shall we use?	**What art work will we use?**
Slogans and catchphrases	

Activities

- Use to organise a brainstorming session about designing a persuasive poster for wearing school uniforms.

- Use the frame to plan own posters.

Term 3
Non-fiction

Persuasive writing
Main focus Model poster (see also page 57)
NLS teaching objective T25

WHICH WOULD YOU RATHER SEE?

DON'T WASTE YOUR VOTE!
TICK FOR SCHOOL UNIFORM TODAY

Activity

- Draw attention to impact of the use of a question to get attention, the bias of the illustration, the brevity of the text, the call to action, etc.